Moonroads

Moonroads

POEMS

Connie T. Braun

CMU PRESS
WINNIPEG, MANITOBA
2025

CMU PRESS

CMU Press
Canadian Mennonite University
500 Shaftesbury Blvd.
Winnipeg MB R3P 2N2
www.cmupress.ca

CMU Press is learning and striving to create an inclusive and welcoming space for people of many identities and communities. We work on land which is the ancestral home of the Anishinaabe, Cree, Dakota, and Métis peoples. We are grateful for their stewardship of this place.

Editor: Sarah Ens
Copyeditor: Sue Sorensen
Design and layout: Jonathan Dyck
Cover art: White Dress (Pleated Skirt), acrylic on canvas, 48 x 48 inches (2015), by Gathie Falk. With the kind permission of Michael Gibson Gallery, London, Ontario.

Printed in Canada by Friesens Corporation, Altona, Manitoba.
ISBN: 978-1-987986-22-8

Library and Archives Canada Cataloguing in Publication

Title: Moonroads : poems / Connie T. Braun.
Names: Braun, Connie T., 1962- author.
Identifiers: Canadiana 20240479092 | ISBN 9781987986228 (softcover)
Subjects: LCGFT: Poetry.
Classification: LCC PS8603.R3819 M66 2025 | DDC C811/.6—dc23

---

for E

my companion on
the moonroads

CONTENTS

EAST

WEST

Gratitude is a scattered
homeless love

ANNA KAMIEŃSKA

all experience is an arch wherethro
Gleams that untraveled world

ALFRED, LORD TENNYSON

The Earth's Two Poles

Just as one map
cannot capture every

glacier's trough,
windblown dune, or rift

beneath a sea,
this one body,

in whom I live and move,
cannot contour home,

yet homes
my being.

Longing and belonging
are the earth's two poles.

NORTH

our migrations
follow an ancient route

Moonroad
(Matrilineal)

How the river shone
in summer, a road of light—there,

on the bank, beneath the willows
my grandfather sat down.

Later, in the saturnine shade
he wept, only after he was able

to return, after every burnt stone
was overturned, the old city

from the rubble rebuilt, his life
reassembled by many children,

no words on his tongue
for such a radiant mourning.

Joy and dolor elide in the heart,
heart, tongue, organ and muscle.

To live, not just endure, requires strength.
How he must have known this

those nights he stood on the bow,
following the moonroad over the water.

My Name
(Patrilineal)

after "My Name"
JOHN MINCZESKI

In 1818 my name migrated
from Prussia to Russia in pursuit
of farmland—planted watermelon, corn,
and potatoes for a century, though hardly
enough to live on, until the promised land

was expropriated,
my name marked
enemy of the people and
placed on a list, forced
to hide in birch forests at night,
black ravens
filling their quotas

for labour camps.
War erupted. Front lines
sliced through our villages. As the snow fell,
my name fled for its life in an open boxcar
strewn with lice-infested straw.

In 1948, my name scrawled
in a Bible handed out to refugees,
on the page of births and deaths;
a survivor.
When the emigration papers
were signed, the final letter,

a doubled *n*, was dropped,
like a stone into the ocean.
Did my name look less foreign
on that converted troopship
still smelling of fresh paint, sailing to Canada
where my name settled
in an unheated garage? My name worked
in the hop-yard, for a few dollars
a day, just enough
to start over. Of the missing consonant,
my father said only one was necessary,
one less heaviness to carry.

Keeping Things Vague

after "Diamonds & Rust"
JOAN BAEZ

On the night of my conception
under the threat of nuclear war,
the Prince of Camelot
spoke in black and white.
After the phospor glow

my father made love to my mother
as if to defy Stalin,
threat lingering.
That Cold War January
I was born with a mark,
a small diamond of rust
above the corner of my mouth.

When I was fourteen he protested
as Joan Baez sang
of diamonds and rust on my LP, curtain of iron between us,
diamonds and rust, for him the same.
"Why don't you understand?"—my mouth,
but with a mole like hers.

When my children had grown,
he asked me to listen.
You are so good with words, he told me,
my father who said nothing
could describe that war,
keeping things vague—
not even history's camera
could capture a true image:
wild lily of the valley,
a white stallion bucking,
riderless, fields
stained red.

First Language

Plainspeak, ordinary, flat *diets,*
these words of my mother
tongue, thick and rich with
cream and butter vowels, consonants
sticking to my teeth and corners
of my mouth like brown sugar,
paska's yeast dough, *zwieback,* crumbs
of cherry and apple *platz,* plum
and apricot *kuchen,* and earthy
nouns and verbs, snap
peas and carrots plucked
or July's raspberries, strawberries
dew-picked,
harvests preserved, put up in jars,
jams, dill-pickle cucumbers zesty
with horseradish and garlic—
without sentiment
from grownup lips, language so simple
in my child-mouth, *how it tasted.*

Bereft of Speech

In the last years, she lapsed back,
back to her child-self running
along the white sand road
calling
for her mother,
her tongue a road
through the village.
Tall grasses
have grown over
the abandoned cemetery where
on one of the stones
my grandmother's
grandmother's
last name, *Kliewer,*
is etched, *Kliewer,* derived
from a word from the north,
klaver, clover, variant
from the Vistula delta, *Platdietsch,* Flat
German, referring to the low-
land, tongue like a river flowing
from Friesland's plains,
plain language without signs, or page,
pages scattered, rustling
tongue

in the wind,
worschle (vorsh-leh),
whisper, Low German
diverging from High, *gefluste,*
the way a river
diverges
when the land is flat.
Verb, *flustern,* to whisper.
Fluss, river. River Vistula,
on the bank, the village, tongues,
Low German, aural
and of the body,
Hunga, hunger.
Wota, water, Vistula's
worschle
through tall grasses, clover, pines
that border the village,
the sand road

wandering
to the last breath.

To Live on in a World

after "Mass of the Moon Eclipse"
DENISE LEVERTOV

The war's umbra
completed its slow passing over the earth

and in that boom and howl, during my first year,
Ginsberg came to Vancouver

with Levertov, poetry
catechising the darkness.

And slowly,
more slowly than desolation overtook,

the return of light. The poets taught
such a laboured return requires attention.

Although they believed in afterlife,
my parents taught me to live on in a world.

Not long ago, I watched as the sun
was consumed by the moon,

crosswise earth, a blackened road.
Attention, faith, alike, I think—waiting

for light. Thin shimmers sufficient
to live through the dying.

Nesting Doll

A floral maroon *platok* covers her head,
cornflowers bloom across her belly, her torso

twists open—more painted dolls spill out—

twelve in all,
birthed in a farmhouse,
four from 1939 to 1945. Wide hips,
empty breasts, her bare
hands, thick and large, the village washwoman,
her labour, forced.
At harvest hoeing potatoes in a stranger's field,
her narrow shoulders bore
heavy
pails, the weight
of dislocation, every simple possession
seized from the wooden cart in the flight.

Love's presence with my hazel eyes,
she looked up at me when I was a girl,
smiled with new teeth. She would not tell me
of scarcity, and I would never guess

that her best dishware was cheap, her table
perpetually set, all the grandchildren
eating cabbage, chicken and *bubbat* with prunes,
cherry *vereniki* rich with butter and cream,
stone-fruit *platz, piroshkies, paska* at Easter and, rising
each Saturday morning, dough for the *zwieback*. Only food

spoke of the past,
but it wasn't the language
for grief. Nesting within,
my childhood, my children: in her floral dress
for Sundays, always an apron,
head bent, headscarf fluttering above
her plentiful garden.

Two Accordions

There is the story of the accordion—sold by a refugee boy to a
man in South America for a wagon and an ox because the man had
always wanted one. I know nothing of that man or

if he could play it or which songs he longed for. Who knows what
the refugee boy bought the accordion with before that. Black market
cigarettes? From an American soldier, perhaps, on his way home
from Berlin, or

did the boy win it in a bet? Less is known about the accordion (a
German-make, a *Hohner*, let's say), only that it sailed from Germany
to South America with the refugee boy. Did he play

it on the ship and is this how the girl he would marry fell in love? I
picture him blond and blue-eyed, a cigarette dangling from his lips,
squeezing out the bellow's breath, pulling in.

Though the boy could play, he would trade it for the chance
to make a start, marry the girl and immigrate to Canada, all
because the man with the wagon and ox had wanted music badly.

There is the story of another accordion—a girl, the seventh of ten
siblings who lived, who arrived, penniless, in Canada where

she worked in the city, saving until she could buy the accordion at
the music store for a hundred dollars. Who sold her the *Roland*
doesn't seem to matter, nor that she couldn't

afford a piano and bought the accordion instead. It was new and
cherry red, and she longed to play an instrument with keys. A
simple polka, or waltz. Her arms push-pulling,

her hair a beehive, drawing the gaze of a handsome darkhaired
young man from the old world. The two spoke the same language
but didn't talk about war,

her slim fingers pressing and folding
songs, and after playing accordion for only a brief time the girl said
yes and sold it to buy a queen-size bed.

Our family stories, bellows emptied, filled.

The Woman Who Lives in the Summer House

after *Lost then Found* (collage and oil)
VICTOR WANG

By the Okanagan Lake's edge,
sour cherry trees grow
for making jam and pies and *vereniki,*
like in Poland, Ukraine. Here in the summer
house, sunflowers bloom, thick
palette-knife-petals behind an unknown
young woman's shoulders. Kerchiefed head,
her turned face, half in shade,
        my grandmother, once young, or my mother,
        my daughter,
full lips closed; her eyes look past
the edge
of canvas.
Beneath the hues
of red and gold,
luminous
pallor of her skin and coarse
cloth of her peasant blouse,
the paint scraped thin,
        a collage of women.
At the cleft in her blouse, her hands
come together, not clasped, or folded,
tips of her fingers touching
as if to cup her heartbeat,
her hands,
thick from unpaid labour,

like my grandmother's were,
but how soft to a child, her hands.
Ripe with remembrance, my lips,
our eyes, dark seeds—
stone within flesh, seed within stone,
          we are stone fruit.

The Builder

In the grainy photograph my father's silhouette
skates the river

behind the house

he built for us, one of many.
Our mother made us homes.

When the ice melts, it leaves no mark on the river,
nothing to remember it,

only the grey image.
But the tree leaves rings in wood. Does a house

remember?
He says *I worry about forgetting.*

He means needing my care. I know
that labour is a form of love. Reliance, a form of trust.

I think of each house.

The ones that held us.

The rivers that flow through our lives.

His, on the steppe, ours, in the valley,
white water, or cloudy with silt.

Uprooted /Braided

i.

I help my mother with the tasks
she finds most difficult,
remove portraits from old frames, pack
photo albums. My aunt empties
kitchen cupboards of Tupperware,
corning ware, and baking pans
darkened with use, for the thrift store.
From her bedroom, my mother calls my name,
says she has something for me
something kept

for fifty years, five moves—
unwrapping the tissue paper
I'm taken back to six,
hairdresser's scissors snipping
my long braid's brown sheen

turned dull—
perhaps she simply hadn't known
what to do with it, holding it
out to me now like a gift. Braid, double-
stranded helix,
soft between my fingers,

then my hand pulls away—

ii.

A little German girl was named for the lettuce her mother loved. The story goes that when pregnant, the mother longed for this lettuce so her husband would sneak into the garden of an enchantress to pick it.
But the price to satisfy is steep.

When Rapunzel turned twelve, the enchantress locked her away. One day a king's son saw Rapunzel in a turret and climbed up her rope of hair. The next time, as he climbed up to her, the enchantress snipped off the girl's braid and the prince plunged into thistles.

The thistles pierced his eyes, and he wandered blind. After a time, one day, recognizing a voice, he followed its sound and found Rapunzel. She held his face between her hands and wept.

Two of her tears fell into his eyes.
The story doesn't say whether sorrow or joy healed his blindness.
Perhaps a tear of each.

iii.

When I was six, my aunt called me Rapunzel after the girl with the braid
whose mother longed for
lettuce, rampion its other name.

Why the mother longed for it so
the fairy-tale doesn't say, but rampion is known for its healing properties.

There is a lesser-known fable about a girl who picks wild rampion in
a field
and discovers
a hidden staircase that descends.

When the girl is an older woman, a rope of her of own hair leads her
back to a field, rampion's mauve bellflowers in full bloom.

Handed Down

Her hands' dorsal sides are spotted, skin thinning,
transparent as the cotton sheets, washed over

and over each week. My mother used to run the clothes
through the wringer, hang the bedding on the line

slung from the house to a pole, a blue cord, hands
pulling the laundry across the yard like a curtain.

I was there too,
rocking in the willow basket

under white sails or pinching
clothespins to fingertips, pretending

at beauty
with such long nails.

Woven handles against her lifeline, my mother
carried her load to clean and fold or mend.

I was born prematurely. Held in the palm of her hand,
she marveled.

When I became a young mother, I claimed the willow basket
(my father made it). When I turned thirty, my mother

gave me her ruby ring, the first she owned
besides her slim wedding band. She used to tell me

I was her closest friend, but I didn't know how
to hold that until my own daughter became a woman

and my longing was the same. When she turned thirty,
I gave my daughter my mother's ring. Finger to finger

to finger, ruby blood drops. My hands,
willow reed bones, chords of blue strung from my heart.

Where My Dad Taught Me to Swim

Keep your head above water he said
as I floundered.

He threw me back in.
Stop struggling he said

so I learned
to let the lake hold me,

though I didn't comprehend anything
about weight and displacement,

not the laws of water,
or of his life,

its hunger, survival.
With his fishing rod, he was content

alone in the jon-boat
out on the lake for hours.

Now I simply close my eyes
and breathe,

float, learn
that ease is not the same

as a lack of hardship.

Coracle

after *Skin Boats* (art installation)
Erica Grimm

Willow
tendons and skins

suspended
on water.

Our migrations
follow an ancient route.

Tendon and skin
carry our grief.

A dim glimmer
rises over the deep.

SOUTH

this body of flesh
sculpted of paradox

Sacred

An only daughter, these six old women are all I know
of sisters. Not saints
though they are being made holy
through the body.

My mother, who still drives, brings chicken soup—
Tilly, salad, Annie, bee-sting cake—
to Emily's house, an hour away,
where Ella and Martha, who both
have difficulty walking, also live.

Emily has had trouble with her vision.
The doctor confirmed it isn't her eyes.
The tumours are many.
Scans have also indicated spots in the sacrum.
The sacred bone.
The bowl-shaped bone
that was once a cradle.

The sternum? My mother must think again.
The bone that shelters the heart.

I think all our bones are sacred,
the last of our remains,

shot through with love and pain.

Bone Cosmology

i. Throughout life there is the breakdown
of bone

and new bone
formation.

270 bones at birth,
206 bones in adulthood.

ii. Cold wind turns bone
to ice.

Skin pierced by bone
is fire.

iii. The ischial bone has wings, humans,
birds, an ilium bone.

All mammals and birds, you and I,
with an iliac bone, largest bone

of the hip, solid butterfly
inside us.

iv. Limb buds, scaffolds for bone.
An infant with soft fontanelle

leaves a permanent record
in her mother's bone.

v. The cranial suture fuses in midlife.
We know things in our bones.

vi. The pain in bone
is a deeper pain.

The ache of the heart is felt
deep within one's bones.

vii. To access the heart,

the breastbone is cleaved,

and the weight of our bones
carries us.

Shadow and Light

Consider an old master's portrait,
a young woman, blushing
areolas, forbidden breasts,
like two small halves of an apple,
plump winged putto
nestled at her feet.
Enviable, though her male creator's
fantasy, how the subject
rests back into
her own body,
dappled in the meadow.

Or consider a statue I suddenly remember:

I was eighteen when I discovered her
in an Amsterdam park beside a canal,
her polished, marble, sturdy legs
filigreed by sunlight through leaves.
It was as if gazing at

my own reflection in the water,

just beginning to see, this body
of flesh sculpted of paradox.

Geography is in Your Bones

My mother drank from it,
dug by her grandfather's hands,
the deep well in Poland,
soil's strontium accumulating
in milk teeth,

tongue pressed against ridges to form sounds
of first language. Perhaps, I first learned it in the womb.
Home, an isotope in deciduous teeth,

geography, in the bones,
ribs, rafters over the heart. Rain seeps through
bedrock and soil, into summer
barley and wheat fields, and garden's yield.

On an August afternoon, a woman wearing a babushka scarf
sets a small, wooden table under a cherry tree,
in its shade, a chair,
checkered cloth, smoothed flat by her hands,

chilled pitcher of juice
pressed from the tree's stone fruit and water
drawn from the well in her yard. She proffers a glass,
minerals of my mother's bones.

The Crossing
(Izmir, 2015)

On the teeming promenade, young couples, children in strollers,
and beyond them,

ferries sailing easily back and forth. We were tourists that spring.
Enticed by the balm of blue shimmering, shops brimming

with carpets, Turkish delights, spices,
and the ruins of churches in fields of red poppies,

we lunched on olives, chicken and apricot tagine, fresh fish
and pomegranate rubies beneath snow-capped mountains

like ones we knew at home,
blinded by the marble steps of Ephesus in the sun,

in the first waves of a war's dispelling. That spring, sipping
local wines, we dined waterside, observing

the promise and loveliness of another's youth. A woman's thigh
in the Aegean, the shape of Lesbos in the distance.

In love's ear

the wood floor recognizes
the weight of you and sighs,

under your hand like a novel's worn page,
the door's latch lifts, a rustle,

warmer than a whisper,
the sound of your approach.

Lingering

From the corner of my eye, a beige streak,
a momentary blur an instant
before we felt the thud on the front passenger side.

She lay unblinking and silent on the gray road.

When the conservation officer arrived, he thanked us
for waiting, *most don't,* he offered as consolation.
Noting the date, he asked if we'd seen a fawn,

the does start giving birth any day now.
He reassures, *it happens often here,*
but her suffering,

her maternal beauty
was not ordinary to me.

Standing a distance away so I could not see
the warden point his gun—
the late morning air
cracked apart.

My whole body shuddered.

There was nothing more to do,
yet, to go,
to just *move on,* I could not
when there seemed a sacred lingering—

Silk

It begins with the silkworm on the mulberry
and grows into a cloudlike whorl
around a pulse

in the darkness. Blonde filaments
spun. In a tenebrous space
the cycle begins

again. A young woman at the wheel
wordlessly spins. Another dyes
each thread a different colour and shade,

every strand placed on the great loom.
I watch the young women, think of
my daughter, her

murky womb

wherein a heart has formed,
nucleus beating a persistent tempo even
before
the embryo fashions around itself

the finished contours of a child.
In the little factory I catch my breath
at the sheen and intricacy of the woven skein

against skin, slight as a sigh, my own heart
beating from before the first breath until
the last is spent—

from beginning
to end,
the threads, the labour of it.

Out of the Depths Appearing

there is nothing more astonishing than a human face
Marilynne Robinson, *Gilead*

Out of the depths appearing,
swimming, or, like an astronaut,

floating from another realm, a world within,
threaded by a filament to her oxygen.

On the sonogram, she sees another
turn and face her,

rehearsing drawn breath,
the otherwise hidden face

appearing like a mystical vision,
mouth, forming an 0.

Water Walking

Amid the mizzle and spit, her first child,
squalled with the gale outside,

a strange tempest self.

Once the rain had died, sunlight pierced
the birthing room.

She, who fashioned human form and knit
a universe,

could not comprehend new-love's
immensity. Miraculous

as a hand that calms a sea,
which, over time, she would learn to do.

Storms Bring Dreams

Your dream reveals your body
is a rough sea.
You begin to drown,
wake up,
heart racing, out of breath,
tell me the next morning
this is my life now.
I say our dreams reveal what we are
made of flesh
bound in wounds
buoyed by joys. And because I'm your mother,
I tell you something you already know—
the same wood that burns
is wood that floats.
My dear, from this wood
you fashion a boat,
are the boat.
Let me tell you again.
That afternoon, there was a storm.
Your father opened the window for me
to let in the gusting wind and I gasped
for it, the pain
like nothing I had known before,
and bore down.

Images of the Heart

Your heart
leaking in the grey firmament beneath your ribs

is rain, the river overflowing
its banks.

Your heart,
a fist,

unfurled hand,
your unborn grandchild,

    cardiac tissue in the mist
    blinking like a distant lighthouse,

on the monitor,
your heart's magma flashing

red,
blue, orange—

white heat, your heart
beneath the probe,

sound
of footsteps through snow.

Narrow Passageway

but every hour is saved
From that eternal silence, something more,
A bringer of new things
ALFRED, LORD TENNYSON, "Ulysses"

I. (Right Atrium)

The thin membrane between life and
what comes after, a valve, and the heart

a portal. I wait on this side
as the operating room

nurse takes you through a doorway
I cannot enter. I'm entering

a tunnel. *I'll see you* I call, call

my old friend who has offered
to wait the hours with me, although
the true interval is solitary.

Beyond the glass in the atrium
it's just another day, but here

time congeals, and I think how

your heart
and lungs
have been turned off,

stopped; you, and I, in a state of limbo.

Bumping against my mind like
the fat fly against the pane, the possibility

of *complications,* but you, the optimist
have secured our future,

and all the necessary signatures
to avoid probate, *just in case.*

My friend reads my silence
the way only an old friend can
and turns to her novel, a romance.

II. (Right Ventricle)

In time we take our stasis to the fifth floor
surgical waiting-room where a woman
waits for her husband, with her friend;
she and I have something in common.
I admire her style—bright lipstick, silk scarf
stylishly wrapped around her head as she pages *Vogue*
—realize
chemo has left her with no eyebrows.

III. (Left Atrium)

Serious young Sikh men on cell phones usher
an old man into the room, trailed
by a young woman, distraught. They cluster
like bees around the patriarch
in a marigold turban, seat him in a chair; strangers,

we hear their loved-one's
surgeon slowly explain *brain trauma—*
survived the surgery but may not survive
the night—hear the girl's
despair.

One of the boys translates the thin line
to the father whose stricken dark eyes seek somewhere
beyond these walls, or veil. He raises his arms
elbows bent, palms together, holds them up as if
before an altar,
his dignified anguish—how difficult
to watch or to look away.

IV. (Left Ventricle)

In time, as planned,
our family arrives. This designated
(private) space so public, we convene
outside the waiting room. My daughter
hands me the baby, weeks old, the touch of him
like the laying on of hands.

Waiting is a portal through
the heart's four chambers. In the obscurity
of the flesh, love gathers us.

And when it's over, the grave
surgeon appears, ascribes the word

uneventful
to the thin and fragile line

that separates your breastbone.

The Ilium Bears Us

Not a record of wrongs,
bones keep an imprint

of our wounds, a spot
on the iliac crest, the mark

of your accident on the winter road
all those years ago—or metastasis? You

and I, with an ilium bone, solid
butterfly within us, bearing

the weight of us,
creatures formed

with wing and blade of bone,
the journey work of a star, blade of grass,

flesh as grass.
A child asks, what is the grass?

I see the child within you,
within you I see our grown sons.

Sexagenarians, you and I, and you
my first love, still,

we do not keep a record
of wrongs, *love bears*

all things,
the ilium bears us

through these waters,
we dip the blade of oar and pull.

EAST

To dwell
means also to abide

extremes of snow and fire

We have always looked to the moon for answers

about tomorrow,

its sphere of radiance
holds beauty

and the certainty
of storms.

A moonbow
signals the coming snow.

Gradations

July will always hold the scent of water.
always this lake,

its gradations—
blue, grey, black,

transparent skin over muscle
and wind churning up lather.

The heart,
composed of water.

As August ends
the wind kicks up.

I come down to the dock
to sit with the fleeting, the constant.

Swept Away

Through the open window, the watering moon,
the lake at 4 am. Dry pines
rustle their limbs, stones sigh on the shore.

My heart is waxing,
and wax.
I hope

for the multiplication of loaves and fishes
and yesterday afternoon I made
fresh bread, *nicoise* salad.

Facing the lake, we opened a bottle
of white, an Okanagan blend,
raised our glasses.

My mother would always exclaim, *now this is living!*
I notice only now
that yesterday she said, simply, *cheers.*

We talked about the forests burning,
and last summer's flood.
How large the willow on the beach has grown, I said.

Do you remember when I buried the dog beneath it? Dad asked.
Last year's flood
swept away the bones.

Shelter Cove

As if a shoreline mist,
smoke from the kindled forest lingers

after last night's blaze, a mountain
red in the dark. We wait for rain

to end or placate the drought.
In this natural realm, wild-

fires are part of living

here, this latest one, no different from
another burning's potential.

To dwell
means to also abide

the extremes of snow and fire.

The Old Douglas Fir

Every year he plants tomatoes,
geraniums, and marigolds,
tender for this climate, and the great Douglas fir
in the yard casts shade.

But now his back aches
and the children are busy
with their own families
and yards, and don't drive

the hours to come as often.
He says he doesn't know why
he's so tired. The fir
drops spiked cones and needles

in the gutters.
He's thought about selling, but
thinks the kids will all
miss this place someday. The fir

hides the sun, its roots
pull up the patio, and he knows,
if not the house,
the tree must soon go.

Look at my flowers he entreats his daughter
as he has every summer,
all these years, and she remembers how
he taught her children

to gut fish in a bucket,
then poured out the water and blood
beneath the old fir
to nourish the annuals.

Thistles

We rise early, take our shovels and rakes, bend
our backs, pull weeds
between the rows. *The cursed ground*

will produce thistles. To eat them, trim the spines.
You will eat the plants of the fields. We pull

tall mullein, yellow flower,
verbascum used for centuries to cure
tuberculosis,

invasive cirsium, Canada Thistle,
so named, but not
of this place.

What is the curse? *Thistles grow in soil*
that has been disturbed. We wrench, remove

roots, stones. Russian Thistle.
Bent low to the ground
there is time to remember.

Mother and father hoed between rows
for survival, and after the war,
young immigrants,

grew raspberries, canes with spines, in a valley drenched
with morning
dew, and beneath the row

the baby drowsed. Slender Flower. Blessed
Milk Thistle. In ground that has been disturbed,

the hint and shade
of purple feed butterflies and bees.
Songbirds feed on the seeds.

Old blooms are dried clusters in the early evening,
but the apple tree is dense,

and I have picked apples for sauce,
like my mother used to prepare,

an heirloom variety,
the tree, tolerant and hardy,

and the fruit, crisp and tart,
keeps only a few days after picking, best for cooking.

My mother and I sit on the porch bench
between the hydrangea's grace and the front door.

I brought my children here each summer,
sprinklers at sunrise, soft

percussion of the day's overture.
Early evening, fragrant with apple, hydrangea and mountains

purpling, fourth movement *pianissimo,*
my apple-box full,

my mother asks, *Do you want more?*

A Minute More

after "At the River Clarion"
MARY OLIVER

The first rays of sun have made it
over the pines, but do not reach

the edge

of the dock. A minute more.
There is someone I love who grows old,

and ill.

Clouds discard
their shadows on the hills.

A lone

duck, brown and plain, bows its head,
wings pressed, and dives

beneath

lake's skin. The light breeze
fingers vellus, my arms,

my face.

Sun rising, summer
drawing to its close, my hand

unfurls.

There is someone I love.
On the water's surface,

rings—

In Lieu of Flowers

Today, words do not make sense,
seem contradictory, like

black flowers:
tulip,

hollyhock, poppy,
cornflower, iris,

and nasturtium
with its bitter taste, sweet scent.

Holy and wordless.

Black tulip
throats open.

Nasturtium
beckons the hummingbird.

A few weeks after the funeral,

she climbs the rocky path, all alone, late
sun tangled in the pines,
valley shadowed, under drifts, lake blackening

below. It's too early for spring.
In the snow,
she steps into a clearing: there,

a stag is watching, eyes

the colour of a young man's shadow,
                                        woods bare, gentle

silence thickening.

Antumbra

Who would not founder in the darkness
of immensity?

Even the moon
can swallow the sun.

Ragged edge,
the cartography

of absence.
Night,

rugged shoreline
lit with phosphorescence.

Even darkness
holds the memory

of light,
eyes closed, a star point behind the lids.

The Plough in Spring

I saw you once again,
for a moment, as I drove by.
Not in this country,

but far away,
lost place,
in the potato field, brown

mare's hide
gleaming, your eyes
shaded by your cap. I was not

mistaken,
sunlight
in my eyes

illuminating you like that,
behind the plough in spring,
not of this earth anymore.

WEST

intercardinal points
guide me

Thundersnow
for Roger

We descend, oblivious.

With my husband, I have flown almost across Canada, invited to
speak about flight
and dispossession.

There is another war in Ukraine.

*

The snow begins to flurry.

At the airport, a car service picks us up.
We settle into the back seat of a black Cadillac, buckle in for the
hour and a half it should take us to our friend's home.

In Toronto a snow squall, the second week of Lent.
In Vancouver, crocuses appear.

We talk about first things.
Our driver's name is Roger.
Roger tells us he has a wife, a small daughter, just one-and-a-half.

Do you speak Arabic?
Roger asks me, and I, a white Canadian woman, answer *no,* wonder
why
he has asked me this.

A later arrival, a half-hour, and we would not have landed.
There are no towns, no street lights, impossible to see

the road ahead only a red line,
cars and transport trucks,
flashers on.

The sky flashes and everything is white.

*

Snow dampens the sound of thunder, despite this lightning
storm's name.

In the warmth of the car, soft jazz. We feel the force of wind, hear
its howl.

Tires grip the thickening layer of snow.
Wipers madly clear a wedge of window.

I'm feeling a little stressed, I say, as Roger leans forward to see.
Roger exhales, exclaims,
Me, too! I have never driven in snow before.
We all laugh. *Well,* I say, *you are doing a very good job.*

We drive, almost blindly, in almost blizzard.

He will be late tonight, his wife will worry. *Of course,* we say, when
he asks
to call her. On the speaker-phone, their voices hushed in another
language.

My husband asks where he is from. *Syria. Aleppo. It snows in Syria,*
  in the mountains.
But not very often in Aleppo, not like this, Roger says.

He came to Canada in 2015, just seventeen, the same age
my father was when he first arrived here in 1947, after years

as a refugee, "stateless," dispossessed
of home and identity.

Oh, the rubble of all the cities.

*

Most will not see thundersnow their entire lifetime.

I saw it once before, from inside, looking into the whiteout.

For Roger, this is the first time;
Roger, from Syria, who has not returned, and because I am here to
  share stories of flight and dispossession, is driving

through the storm.

He does not talk about his past.
Tells us, instead, *it is not good*
in Syria. The recent earthquake in February left so many dead.

People still buried in the wreckage.

Cousin and cousin's wife, both twenty-one, were just married.
They were very happy. Married one month. They are both dead.

Snow impedes the rescue operations. This winter has been one of
the coldest.
Children without winter clothes.

*

Hours after expected, Roger delivers us to our friends,
driveway shoveled, entry light on, front door open.
We are beckoned inside.

I can't stop thinking about him driving back to Toronto, his wife
and daughter.
After an hour I ask my husband to call.

Roger answers surprised, so happy.
We want to know, are you almost home?
Soon!

I pray for your safety, I say. *Thank you, thank you,* he exclaims.

*

It is the second week of Lent, a season, in my tradition, of remembrance.

Easter, from Friday to Sunday, dispossession to return.

My father returned twice, the first time when the iron curtain fell.
Again in summer 2005, along with me, my children.
Lightning over the steppe. He remembered snow in Zaporizhzhia.

Over eight million people displaced from Ukraine.
And how many now dead?

As I speak of flight and dispossession, other descendants share stories.

I tell them that a man from Syria brought me safely through the storm.

Intercardinal Points

Marked by the celestial,

I return,
I return.

And the dead shine on
though my naked
eye cannot see.

White star, azimuth,
my true bearing

across the arc of the natural world.

Magnetic north, zero degrees, magnetic south
constantly shifting,

cardinal directions
indicate the general site
of home; intercardinal points
guide me more precisely.

Breath
for Judy

I had been waiting for your news.

A blast,
knocking
against the large window:

the harbour's white-tipped waves,
the maple leaves red-turned-brown
on the pavement like fallen gloves
from your mother's thin, veined hands.
September passed quickly

and yet, the waiting. The waiting.

I had not gone to church when you called.
It was peaceful, you said.
That's always the prayer.

But that it should come without warning
or trumpet sounding—

at her bedside
you held your breath,
as if to be sure, listening,

before beginning to make the calls.

And I wonder at
the wind
hovering
over the water,
the timing of it at my window.

The last exhale—

pneuma,

its knocking,

its tearing
from our hands,

its wake.

A Beam to Travel On

after *Book of Mercy* "19"
LEONARD COHEN

As they hug goodbye, one last photograph.

Son with the name of an explorer,
ending in a consonant like a backbone,
is much taller than his mother,

his hair catching the light like a moon
and on sturdy shoulders the world

in a back-pack. Essentials for his odyssey:
Nikon camera, wide-angle lens, and clear-
mindedness, a compass to navigate
these hazy years.

As he walks away to board his flight, he turns,
a wide, open-lipped latitude

curved across his face—joy,
a beam to travel on.

Promise

Silvered leaves of olive groves fade, a mirage
in snow. From Syria, how could this man,
willing to sacrifice everything for the children,
know such a place
as Lethbridge, Alberta, existed?

Their futures are more important than my memories.

Three years in flight, now this
bungalow, and growing here,
a juniper shrub.

What matters is that there is a place for all.

Porch light glows in the frozen night. A family
of deer in the front yard. Stars in a silent sky.

Safety is home.

Even in the language
he must give up, can't find the words.
His wife tries to hand him the phone.
Eyelids squeezed shut, he signals her to tell them
he's busy, fingers to lips
pretending to smoke until, at last,

he can speak. When it's time to say goodbye
he believes—or pretends to—

We will come visit you, God willing.

Today, the wings of a dragonfly graze her,

once in Times Square, and again, leaving
the matinee on Broadway,

Burn This. The characters grieve, try
to make sense of their lives.

Today, her birthday, daughter
with mother, two women

in New York City.
She had been here years before with her

aspirations. This is the first time since giving birth
that she is away from her children, her lifelines,

her lifeless marriage.
The throb

of a dragonfly large as a hummingbird
amid the crowd crossing Fifth Avenue,

hovers—a third time.
White sun, a spotlight,

finger-long wing
touches the slope of her shoulder.

She stops, stands motionless in the middle of Fifth,

iridescent in the light.
A dragonfly emerges

from under the water; a nymph,

sheds her casings in stages,
takes to the air.

Bespoke

Her youngest son has learned to gauge the length
it takes to go the distance,

to fashion a framework for the way he is made.
Philosophy and craft in hand,

he measures height, reach of arm, inseam, and torso,
as if a tailor. She used to mark his height

each year on the wall. Now she comes to him
as she attempts a steep grade. The road ahead, a seam

between sky, land; a ride,
or a labour. In his shop, the dog follows him with her eyes.

Afterwards they to walk to the coffee shop next door.
What kind of riding do you want to do?

City, road, leisure, distance? he asks. She says, *I'll ride alone,*
or with your father.

Just then her phone rings and her son sees that it's him,
reaches across the table, turns the ringer to silent.

But what experience are you hoping for? he persists,
opening his notebook to sketch,

new, slim band on his finger, already figuring it out.

Timepieces

We bought it a decade ago to mark the end
of a career, the beginning of something new
for us, and it occurs to me now that we celebrate
significances with wristwatches—

the kids' graduations, an anniversary, retirement.
Now we look at another timepiece, examine quality
material, design—which of two will be the right one?
Diameter of each, the same as your pearl-faced Rolex,

circumference of your aorta, to be tucked into your
open chest. *The mechanical one, unlike a biological valve,*
the surgeon says, *you'll always hear ticking.* Even before
surgery, I sense the tempo of the tremulous long hand.

Sitting across from him, as if desk a jewellery counter,
he, a horologist, we are buying time.

Looking Back

I always look in the rear-view mirror or over my shoulder.
These are not figures of speech.

You were driving slow,
thick slush on the road.

At home, I was in my second trimester with our first son.
Within my body I have carried gratitude

and grief simultaneously.

The truck slid over the side of the mountain.
Another woman's husband, another mother's son.

I feel sorry for the things I cannot control,

the little boy who ran away from home
on bicycle, the young man who dropped out

to work in a silver mine, a dark place

that nearly killed you.
You saved a man's life in the blast.

After your open-heart surgery, people asked you
what you would change.

You said there is nothing
you can do about the past.

There is the picture of us, not yet married,
hiking above the snowline.

Most days I overlook that it is the same mountain.

Throughout our marriage, behind our home, this mountain
in the east, often obscured,

but when the clouds break,
it is unbearable

to not look back.

You fill my glass, I drink from yours.

You arrange your finds by colour, region,
varietal, write out tags with price and year to slip
around the necks, keep a spreadsheet
of daily drinkers and those for the future,
listen to panels of experts.
This is growing
into a more serious pursuit.
When a particular French wine
on my last birthday delighted me, you bought crates,
some Bordeaux and Burgundies
to drink in five years, the others
in ten, you said.
French. Italian, Australian,
Portuguese, Spanish, Chilean,
all the places we've been.
When I open a bottle
without paying attention,
Château Grand-Puy Ducasse, Pulliac, 2010,
you laugh and say it was a keeper.
Then ask how I like it.
There are days I wonder
if we should be drinking wine at all.
I need reassurances. You've never been one to worry.
Researchers have found no association
between moderate consumption of red wine and the risk
of developing prostate cancer. You are a "big red" guy.
You say Super Tuscans upset the purists.

You love the blends. But the Brunello
is for me, the only Tuscan
with just one grape.
You fill my glass.
I drink from yours,
forgetting where I put my mine.
Our cups holds many seasons,
the way we do. Next year
we will plant our own vines, *pinot noir,* you say.
We listen to a panel of experts.
T numbers, PSA values, Gleason patterns and volume,
another science we are learning.
Patients can choose from different options.

Hidden by Clouds

after "Witness"
Denise Levertov

i.

Pastoral valley,
border crossing,
narrow pass
where the tide rushes in.
The road through my childhood has led me here.

Geography, metaphor,
behind me the mountain,
its snow nimbus even in summer, icon
in the shadow of the valley. The church
named after its view, a reminder
of where to look in times of trouble.

And here, her sister mountain,
luminous. Although cloaked in clouds I know
she is here.

*

Awe, a mountain thrust towards sky,
awe, noun and verb,
an open mouth.
You don't have to seek it. It rises

from your chest
and throat. A roar,

or whisper. Fire in a woodstove.

ii.

All day the mountain hid.

On the bush, snowberries,
at the foot of cedars, moss carpet.
Indian plum.
The fir tree,

two separate trunks entwined,
then fused into one
after the struggle, like a long-married couple
(and I thought, yes, love is like this).

Roots, arms and fingers
reaching out,
all the trees
connected beneath.

In the afternoon, a robin in another fir's crown
called out, feathers
crimson, each of us noticing
the waning light

a little longer than the day before.

Behind a thin veil
of cloud, the face
of moon.

*

To keep the fire burning, I feed it. Paper.
Kindling. Split wood.
It blazes, smolders. Tending the fire

is a spiritual practice.

In darkness,
between night and morning, I wait.
No. Expect. Something. I can't find
words. But it is here,

a mountain I cannot see.

iii.

Arrival of sunlight
illumines ferns,
pours
onto cedar trunks,
spills
through arms, outstretched,
light inching
upwards. There is still a fire
in the woodstove from last night,

and ashes.

In this forest, no willows
like those that lined the edges of rivers,
a past life.
Forests hold our stories,

connect us, root to root;

refuge and pathways,
across borders, generations.

My places of refuge,
a clearing, an open sky.

*

The gravel path through the woods leads
past gardeners pruning grapevines

to the water. I want to see
the snow-capped peak
rising.

Blue, dazzling and swept
of yesterday's webs,
bites my lungs.

An eagle swims sky. The span
of wings,
a crossbeam. I walk past

the construction of a new house,

and through an opening
in the padlocked fence,
past the deer pond to the dazzling sound.
Everything is sea and sky

and I say *thank you*. Beyond,
enrobed in white, immortal,

the mountain
gazing at *me* and I am
no longer hidden by clouds.

Evacuation Alert

The lake breathes,

wrestles with its own depths and lashes
out in late August. There are storms here,

in this valley, house, bed. Thunder rolls
over the mountain, tendon and bone,

your body asleep, your breath
like water, and soothing to me after all,

so I let the night cover us for a while
and do not throw back the sheets to wander.

In the morning there will be smoke
on the water. Like fog, nothing is certain.

Over time we have practiced forgiveness.
There is a piano in our house the children

no longer play. I save the past, or is it
the other way?

Ours was a young marriage
in February. There was snow.

We dreamed of building
from timber and stone,

a solid home. Here on the shore,
it's fire season.

Sparks set the mountains ablaze, the pines
candle, smolder. I know now

what I would leave behind, what I
run toward.

ACKNOWLEDGEMENTS

To live a writing life is both a solitary and shared enterprise. I have my life partner, Erwin, to thank for coming alongside me, and for stepping back, a dance over time. And there are others, poets, teachers, who leave their indelible traces: Sarah Klassen at the first School of Writing at CMU in 2007, Ann Hostetler and Julia Kasdorf at a lake in Minnesota so long ago, my MFA thesis advisor Susan Musgrave, poets Robin Davidson, Carolyn Forché, Kaaren Kitchell, Susan Landgraf, and Lisa Morano (the Forest Sisters) since 2018, Lorna Crozier in recent years, and Lise Goett. And always, Lynn Szabo. To Sue Sorensen and CMU Press for believing that this book belongs, and for making this experience working with you so wonderful, my deep gratitude and appreciation. Sarah Ens, brilliant poet, you are a dream editor! Gathie Falk's exquisite art graces the cover; I am so delighted. Thank you, Jonathan Dyck, for the gorgeous cover and book design. I thank my family and friends for home and belonging. You are all present here, along with my love for the places, land and lake, I have called home.

Versions of the following poems were previously published in the chapbook *Narrow Passageway* (Alfred Gustav Press, 2017):

- "A Beam to Travel on" was published as "China Easter Air"
- "Images of the Heart"
- "Out of the Depths Appearing" was published as "At 19 Weeks"
- "Timepieces"
- "Silk" was published as "A Tenebrous Space"

"My Name" has appeared in the following publications:

- *Force Field: 77 Women Poets of British Columbia*. Edited by

Susan Musgrave. Mother Tongue, 2013.

- *150+ Canada's History in Poetry*. Edited by Judy Gaudet. Acorn Press, 2018.
- *In/Words Magazine and Press:* Refuge(e) special issue (February 2017).

"My Name" and "The Plough in Spring" were published in *Unspoken: An Inheritance of Words,* Fern Hill Publications, 2014 (private limited edition) and 2016 (2nd edition).

"In Lieu of Flowers" and "A few weeks after the funeral" appeared in *Force Field: 77 Women Poets of British Columbia,* edited by Susan Musgrave, Mother Tongue, 2013.

"Moonroad" (originally titled "Mangata"), commissioned for the DaCapo Chamber Choir under the direction of Leonard Enns, was performed as "Following the Moon Road," Christine Donkin, composer, in Kitchener in March 2019. The poem also appeared in *Hamilton Arts and Letters,* vol. 13, no. 2 (2020).

"Geography is in Your Bones" was published in *Nimrod International Journal,* vol. 67, no. 2 (Refuge issue, Spring/Summer 2024).

"The Ilium Bears Us" was published in *Room,* vol. 47, no. 3 (Bodies issue, Fall 2024).

NOTES

The book's first epigraph is from "Gratitude" by Anna Kamieńska. *Astonishments: Selected Poems of Anna Kamieńska,* edited and translated by Grażyna Drabik and David Curzon, Paraclete Press, 2007.

The book's second epigraph is from "Ulysses" by Alfred, Lord Tennyson, as is the epigraph in the poem "Narrow Passageway." The poem, published in *Poems* (1842), is in the public domain.

My Name
The poem "My Name" by John Minczeski is in his collection *The Spiders,* New Rivers Press, 1979.

Keeping Things Vague
Joan Baez's album *Diamonds & Rust* was released by A & M Records in 1975.

To Live on in a World
Epigraph is from "Mass of the Moon Eclipse" by Denise Levertov, *This Great Unknowing: Last Poems,* New Directions, 1999.

The Woman Who Lives in the Summer House
The painting evoked is *Lost and Found,* oil and collage on canvas, by Victor Wang (born 1956) and is in the author's private collection. His work can be found at victorwang.net.

Coracle

The poem refers to the installation *Skin Boats* by Erica L. Grimm (born 1959). Her work can be viewed at ericagrimm.com.

Out of the Depths Appearing

The line in the epigraph is from Marilynne Robinson's novel *Gilead* (Farrar, Straus and Giroux, 2004) and is spoken by the character John Ames.

The Ilium Bears Us

Lines in italics reference Walt Whitman's "Song of Myself" and "A Child said What is the Grass," in *Leaves of Grass* (various editions, 1856–1889), in the public domain. The lines in italics in the penultimate tercet reference 1 Corinthians 13.7.

A Minute More

Lines in italics reference Mary Oliver's "At the River Clarion" in *Devotions: The Selected Poems of Mary Oliver*, Penguin Random House, 2017.

Promise

Lines in italics were spoken by Canadian newcomer from Syria, Mr. Farwan, interview with Adrienne Arsenault, on CBC TV's *The National*, Tuesday 31 May 2016.

A Beam to Travel On

The title and line in italics are from Leonard Cohen's poem "19," in *Book of Mercy*, McClelland & Stewart, 1984.

ABOUT THE AUTHOR

Connie Braun's family immigrated to British Columbia, to the Sumas Prairie, and she was born and raised in Clearbrook, which no longer exists. She lived in Abbotsford before moving to Vancouver and, throughout her life, has spent time in the Okanagan.

The places she has called home are located on the traditional ancestral unceded shared territory of the xʷməθkʷəy̓əm (Musqueam), the Sḵwx̱wú7mesh (Squamish), and Sel̓íl̓witulh (Tsleil-Waututh) Nations; the Sumas First Nation and Matsqui First Nation; and ancestral unceded lands of the Syilx/Okanagan People.

MA, MFA, poet, author of non-fiction, instructor of creative writing, Connie has involvements and interests that span arts, education, social justice, and peace, and (more recently) a small vineyard, pursuits that seem a perfect blend. Her publications include the memoir *The Steppes are the Colour of Sepia* (Ronsdale) and the creative non-fiction book *Silentium: And Other Reflections On Memory, Sorrow, Place, and the Sacred* (Wipf and Stock). Her poetry appears in journals and anthologies and has been set to music. She and Erwin enjoy hiking trips, train travel, exploring wine regions, and spending time with their children and grandchildren.